A JOURNEY WITH HERNÁN CORTÉS

LISA L. OWENS

LERNER PUBLICATIONS ◆ MINNEAPOLIS

Content Consultant:
Sarah Chambers, PhD, History, University of Wisconsin, Madison
Professor in the Department of History, University of Minnesota

Lerner Publications Company
A division of Lerner Publishing Group, Inc.
241 First Avenue North
Minneapolis, MN 55401 USA

For reading levels and more information, look up this title at
www.lernerbooks.com.

Main body text set in AvenirLTPro 12/18.
Typeface provided by Linotype AG.

Library of Congress Cataloging-in-Publication Data

Names: Owens, L. L., author.
Title: A journey with Hernán Cortés / Lisa L. Owens.
Description: Lerner Publications : Minneapolis, 2017. | Series: Primary
    source explorers | Includes bibliographical references and index.
Identifiers: LCCN 2016002986 (print) | LCCN 2016005139 (ebook) | ISBN
    9781512407778 (lb : alk. paper) | ISBN 9781512410983 (eb pdf)
Subjects: LCSH: Cortés, Hernán, 1485–1547—Juvenile literature. |
    Mexico—History—Conquest, 1519–1540—Juvenile literature. |
    Mexico—Discovery and exploration—Spanish—Juvenile literature. |
    Conquerors—Mexico—Biography—Juvenile literature. | Explorers—
    Mexico—Biography—Juvenile literature. | Explorers—Spain—
    Biography—Juvenile literature.
Classification: LCC F1230.C35 O94 2017 (print) | LCC F1230.C35 (ebook) |
    DDC 972.02092—dc23

LC record available at http://lccn.loc.gov/2016002986

Manufactured in the United States of America
1-39349-21161-10/25/2016

CONTENTS

 = Denotes primary source

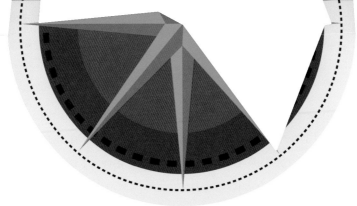

INTRODUCTION
AN IMPRESSION
OF MEXICO

In a 1519 letter to King Charles V, Spanish explorer Hernán Cortés shared details from his Mexican expedition. He told of Mexico's "fertile plains" and "beautiful river banks." He described the country's inhabitants as "people of middle size, with bodies and features well proportioned." A letter like this is considered a primary source. A primary source is a document, image, map, or other object created by a person at the time in which that person lived.

Cortés had never been to Mexico before his expedition.

Cortés left Spain in 1504 and began his exploration of Mexico's geography and people in 1519. The explorer is shown in this nineteenth-century engraving.

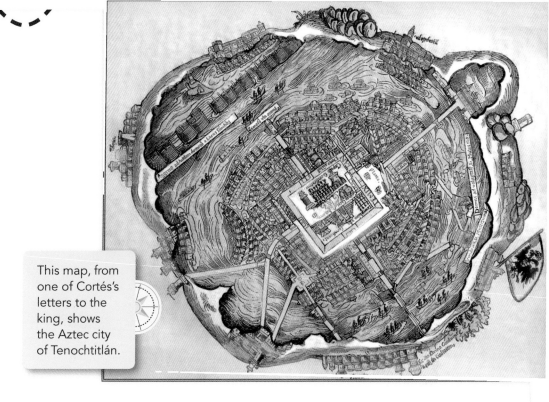

This map, from one of Cortés's letters to the king, shows the Aztec city of Tenochtitlán.

He had no idea how it might differ from his native Spain. But part of his job was to learn everything he could about the place. Knowing Mexico's geography and being able to communicate with its people were important for carrying out his mission to claim the land for Spain. And Cortés stayed in touch with the king to tell him about his findings and the mission's progress.

Cortés's writings give important insight into his own thoughts and actions. Without them, we would still be able to learn about Cortés from primary sources such as diaries and artworks created by others of his time. But his firsthand accounts are a valuable piece of the primary sources puzzle. Historians rely on many different kinds of primary sources to study events and people and to present the most accurate information possible.

This modern photo shows the walls of the castle in Medellín, Spain.

CHAPTER 1
CORTÉS'S YOUTH

In about 1485, Hernán Cortés was born in the town of Medellín, Spain. His parents were Martin Cortés, who was once an army captain, and Catalina Pizarro Altamirano. Martin's ancestry and military record meant the Cortéses were hidalgos, or members of the Spanish lower nobility. They were not rich, but the family owned a bit of land. And they were well-respected in town. Both of Cortés's parents were generous and honest.

As a child, Cortés was often sick. Yet he enjoyed seeking adventure with other boys in his village. They climbed the cliffs around their homes, ran around town, and kicked leather balls back and forth in open fields. Kids at that time enjoyed acting out war games behind the walls of the local castle. There, Christians had conquered Medellín from its Muslim rulers in 1234, as part of a long war that continued in southern Spain until 1492. Children in Cortés's time had grown up hearing stories of the war.

At the age of fourteen, Cortés went to the University of Salamanca. His father hoped Cortés would become a lawyer, which he thought was "the richest and most honorable career of all." Cortés "was very intelligent and clever in everything he did," but he was restless at school. He ignored his studies and dropped out after just two years.

This image shows a page from the book *Las Siete Partidas* (Seven-Part Code), which was the Spanish code of law Cortés may have studied in school. This code of law went into effect in 1348. It included information about the rights of masters and slaves in Spanish society. In the sixteenth century, many of these laws also spread to the New World.

Once back in the family home, Cortés became restless. He would argue with his parents and sometimes get into fights in the village. Eventually, he started looking for opportunities to go out on his own. News of Christopher Columbus's explorations in the Western Hemisphere had by then spread to Medellín. Cortés wanted to see the New World that everyone was talking about. Soon he had the chance to go with family acquaintance Nicolás de Ovando on a 1502 voyage to the Americas. Ovando had been appointed governor of the Indies, and Cortés thought he might find good opportunities there.

News of Columbus's explorations in the New World inspired Cortés to embark on his own journey. This image of Christopher Columbus and his men was created long after their expedition.

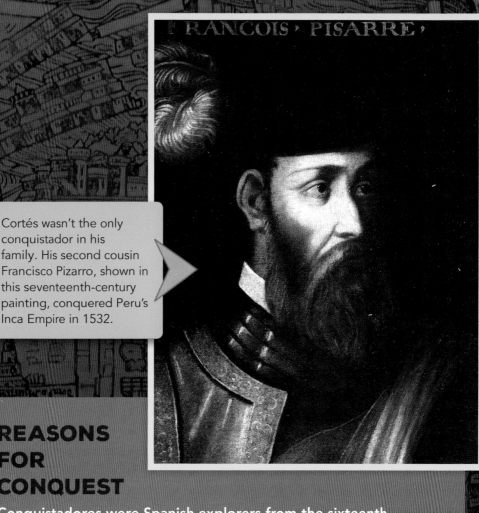

FRANCOIS · PISARRE ·

Cortés wasn't the only conquistador in his family. His second cousin Francisco Pizarro, shown in this seventeenth-century painting, conquered Peru's Inca Empire in 1532.

REASONS FOR CONQUEST

Conquistadores were Spanish explorers from the sixteenth century who took control of newly discovered lands. They did it to increase Spain's reputation and power, spread the Christian faith, and gain wealth for their country and for themselves.

Cortés is best known for leading the Spanish conquest of Mexico. He destroyed the Aztec Empire and claimed its land for Spain. One of Cortés's men, Bernal Díaz, wrote a book about the conquest called *The True History of the Conquest of New Spain*. In it he explains that he joined Cortés's mission because he wanted "to serve God and His Majesty, to give light to those who were in darkness, and to grow rich, as all men desire to do."

Not long before he was scheduled to sail with Ovando, Cortés sprained his back trying to climb over a wall after visiting a young lady. The injury was bad enough that he had to be carried home. He could not make his planned journey.

After a months-long recovery, he was ready to leave home. He spent the next year wandering Spain with little money and no clear plan. Finally, he again decided it was time to see the New World. He visited his parents, and they gave him enough money for passage to the Indies.

In 1504 nineteen-year-old Cortés sailed to the Caribbean island of Hispaniola. The explorer Bartholomew Columbus—a brother of Christopher Columbus—had founded the first permanent Spanish settlement there in 1496. Cortés spent the next several

Bartholomew Columbus, Christopher Columbus's younger brother, was also an explorer for Spain.

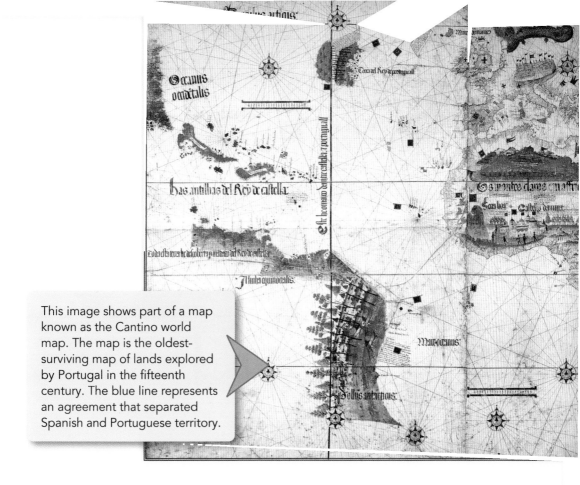

This image shows part of a map known as the Cantino world map. The map is the oldest-surviving map of lands explored by Portugal in the fifteenth century. The blue line represents an agreement that separated Spanish and Portuguese territory.

years supervising the laborers on his farm and serving as a notary in the town of Azua. As a notary, he had to learn about Spanish property rights. This knowledge would become useful in his future career as a conquistador.

An eighteenth-century painting depicts Cortés and Velázquez.

CHAPTER 2
A CONQUISTADOR IN THE MAKING

In Hispaniola, Cortés helped Conquistador Diego Velázquez fight rebellions by Native peoples. When Velázquez received permission to launch a 1511 expedition to conquer Cuba, Cortés joined the effort as a soldier. The mission was successful. Velázquez became Cuba's new governor. He made Cortés his secretary.

Cortés quickly settled into his new life. He was good at his job, and the government rewarded him for it. He was given land and slaves who farmed and worked the gold mines for him. His slaves were the people who had originally lived in Cuba when Spain took it over. Cortés was also given a house in the new Cuban capital of Santiago, where Velázquez later appointed him to two terms as mayor.

In about 1514, Cortés was expected to marry Catalina Xuárez after she publicly announced she'd chosen him. But Cortés was also seeing another Xuárez sister. He liked both women and, finally, refused to marry Catalina. She sued him for breaking his promise. She said that she had been wronged by Cortés, and several witnesses agreed.

This refusal angered Velázquez, who had introduced Cortés to the Xuárez family. He ordered Cortés to go through with the wedding because it was the right thing to do. When Cortés said no, the governor threw him in jail. But Cortés escaped twice.

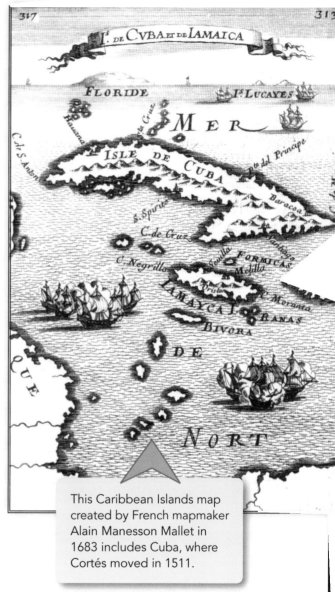

This Caribbean Islands map created by French mapmaker Alain Manesson Mallet in 1683 includes Cuba, where Cortés moved in 1511.

A sixteenth-century engraving shows indigenous laborers working in a mine in Cuba. The image comes from a 1575 book written by André Thevet, who traveled around the world and gathered information about the people and places he encountered.

GETTING AROUND THE LAW

During earlier Spanish expeditions to Mexico, soldiers had captured indigenous people and brought them back to Cuba. They were forced to work at sugar plantations, gold mines, and cattle ranches.

By any other definition, those people were enslaved. But the Spanish Crown—another way of saying "the office of the king"—was against slavery, so Velázquez came up with a different way to use indigenous labor. First, he made official payments for each of the captured laborers and assigned them to various Spanish citizens. Then those Spaniards took legal responsibility for the laborers. This meant they agreed to keep them safe, help them learn Spanish, and teach them about Christianity.

This system, called *encomienda*, was based on similar tactics that had been used in Europe for centuries. The idea behind it was that the stronger people (in this case, the conquerors) protected the weaker ones as long as they served them.

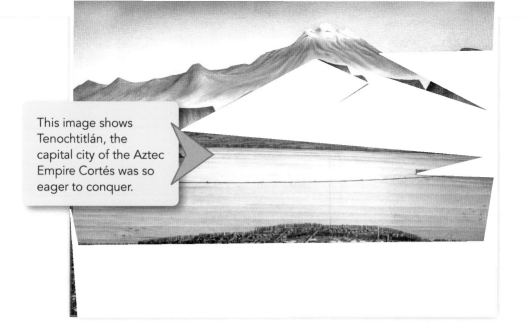

This image shows Tenochtitlán, the capital city of the Aztec Empire Cortés was so eager to conquer.

While on the run after his second escape, Cortés developed a plot against Velázquez. He'd kept records of the governor's dishonest dealings. If things didn't go his way, Cortés planned to expose the details. He met with some other Spaniards who felt the governor had cheated them out of land and slaves. They would speak out if Cortés needed them to.

Then, about a year after the canceled wedding, Cortés made a surprise visit to Velázquez at his country home. The men talked and settled some of their differences. Cortés married Catalina after all because he knew it was good for his reputation. And he never exposed the information he'd collected about Velázquez.

In 1518 Velázquez offered Cortés a key mission. He would be the captain general on an expedition to Mexico. Cortés signed his contract on October 23. His job was to examine Mexico's eastern coast and learn more about Mexican trade practices.

But Cortés had something even bigger on his mind. He had heard stories of the rich Aztec Empire in central

Mexico. Cortés and other Spaniards were eager to see—and conquer—this culture.

Cortés then was about thirty-three years old. He was very ambitious. He took his new position and his reputation seriously. He wanted to make the most of his assignment. He rounded up ships and supplies and recruited men to serve under him. Appearances mattered a great deal to him, and he dressed and acted his part: "He had tailors make him a velvet cloak with tassels of gold, as befitted a prospective lord. In public he kept himself armed and had an escort."

A sixteenth-century image shows a Spanish ship, known as a caravel, flying the red cross flag of Santiago. Caravels were fast ships often used for carrying supplies. Cortés probably used similar ships for his expedition to Mexico.

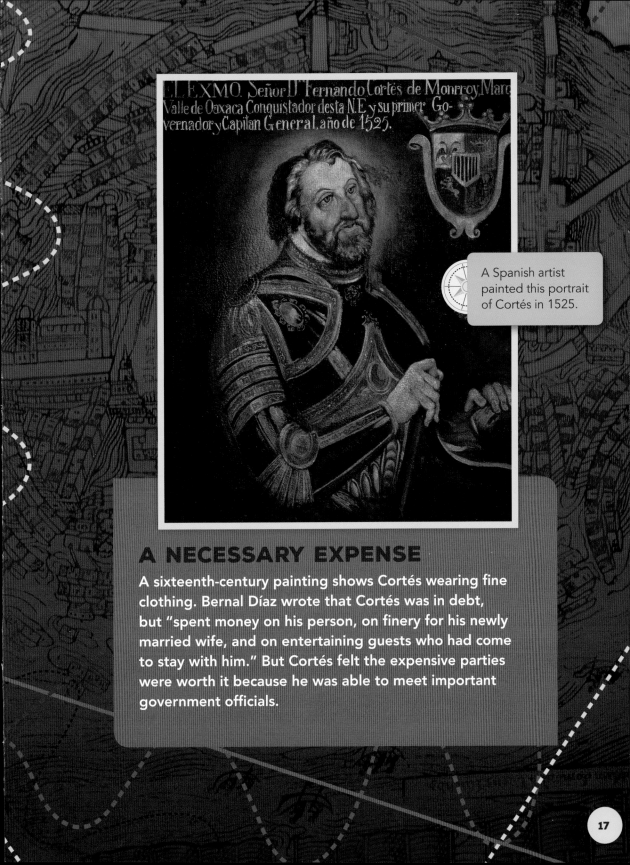

ELEXMO. Señor Dⁿ Fernando Cortés de Monrroy Marq Valle de Oaxaca Conquistador desta N.E. y su primer Governador y Capitan General, año de 1525.

A Spanish artist painted this portrait of Cortés in 1525.

A NECESSARY EXPENSE

A sixteenth-century painting shows Cortés wearing fine clothing. Bernal Díaz wrote that Cortés was in debt, but "spent money on his person, on finery for his newly married wife, and on entertaining guests who had come to stay with him." But Cortés felt the expensive parties were worth it because he was able to meet important government officials.

Meanwhile, Velázquez had a change of heart. He suspected that Cortés wouldn't obey his instructions. He even feared his friend might go to war against the rich Aztecs. Velázquez did want to conquer the Aztecs, but he didn't want all the credit to go to Cortés. So he decided to replace Cortés with someone he trusted to more closely follow his orders.

But Cortés heard rumors of the governor's plan and decided to leave early. He left Havana on November 18, 1518. Some reports say he sailed in the middle of the night before Velázquez could try to stop him.

A nineteenth-century wood engraving depicts Cortés's fleet of ships sailing to Mexico. This image was created long after Cortés's expedition, so it is not considered a primary source.

Because the expedition left so quickly, they had to stop along the way to continue gathering men, weapons, and other supplies. They would need a large, well-equipped army once they reached Mexico. Velázquez kept sending word for Cortés to return. But Cortés ignored the orders at every port.

By early 1519, Cortés's fleet was fully prepared for the final leg of its sea voyage. Bernal Díaz listed their supplies, which included the following:

- eleven ships in all, including one that carried only supplies
- more than five hundred soldiers
- an estimated one hundred sailors, shipmasters, and pilots
- thirty-two crossbowmen
- thirteen musketeers
- sixteen horses
- brass guns, cannons, and ammunition

In March 1519, the expedition landed at Tabasco and seized the area for Spain. A Native woman known as Malinche became one of Cortés's trusted interpreters. With her help, Cortés interviewed the local people. He wanted to find out whatever he could about the land and any enemies he might encounter. He learned that many indigenous tribes hated and feared the Aztecs. Cortés was able to persuade some of them to join his forces.

A nineteenth-century Mexican engraving depicts Malinche.

AN IMPORTANT ALLY

Malinche was also known as Malintzin, in the Aztec language, and Doña Marina, in Spanish. She originally came to Cortés as a slave. But she knew Mayan and Aztec languages, and she quickly learned Spanish. So she became very important to the expedition. Malinche allowed Cortés and his men to communicate with many groups of people. This allowed them to travel safely through Native communities and gain allies. Many people think Malinche was a traitor to her people. Others say she is a hero. In any case, she holds a central role in the history of Mexico.

This nineteenth-century engraving shows Cortés's fleet of ships sinking. Some accounts say Cortés ordered his men to burn the boats. But Cortés's letters and Díaz's writings say that Cortés scuttled his boats, which means he put holes in them so they sank.

Meanwhile, a few of Cortés's men were having second thoughts. They felt loyal to Velázquez and wanted to leave the expedition. They planned to steal one of the ships and return to Cuba. But Cortés was one step ahead of them. He damaged his own ships, causing them to sink. The soldiers had no choice but to stay with Cortés.

This sixteenth-century painting by an Aztec artist depicts Cortés's arrival in Tenochtitlán as he is greeted by a messenger from the city.

CHAPTER 3
THE FALL OF THE AZTEC EMPIRE

Soon the troops began their march from the Gulf of Mexico to Tenochtitlán, the capital of the Aztec Empire. Along the way, Cortés and his men met many Native peoples. Some joined the expedition to conquer the Aztecs. Others battled with the Spanish conquistadores. Cortés convinced the people of the Mexican city Tlaxcala to be his allies. And he seized the city of Cholula for his king. Stories of these conquests spread to other areas, and some cities surrendered instead of fighting what they knew would be a losing battle.

On November 8, 1519, the expedition reached Tenochtitlán. The Aztecs knew Cortés and his men were coming. Crowds

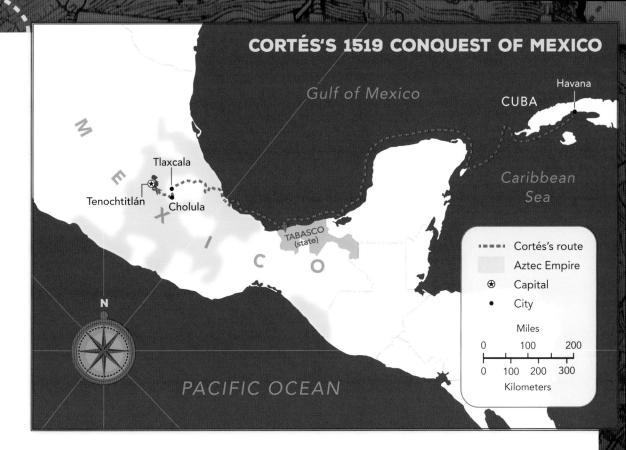

CORTÉS'S 1519 CONQUEST OF MEXICO

Gulf of Mexico

Havana

CUBA

Caribbean Sea

MEXICO

Tlaxcala

Tenochtitlán

Cholula

TABASCO (state)

N

PACIFIC OCEAN

Cortés's route
Aztec Empire
⊛ Capital
• City

Miles
0   100   200
0   100   200   300
Kilometers

gathered to watch Cortés march into their beautiful city. Tenochtitlán was on an island, and Cortés and his men marched there on a wide causeway. He arrived with his army, about a thousand allies, and their horses.

Aztec emperor Montezuma II waited for Cortés and his men on a covered cushion carried by servants. He wore a golden helmet topped with hundreds of brightly colored feathers from tropical birds. At the city's entrance, he welcomed Cortés. The two exchanged gifts of jewelry. Malinche interpreted the emperor's speech. Cortés tried to offer Montezuma a hug, which was a Spanish custom, but he was stopped by the emperor's attendants. This sort of contact with the ruler was not allowed.

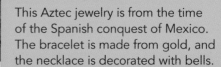
This Aztec jewelry is from the time of the Spanish conquest of Mexico. The bracelet is made from gold, and the necklace is decorated with bells.

AZTEC SOCIETY

The Aztec society was broken up into different classes, including the ruling, upper and lower, military, merchant, priest, and slave classes. The Aztec dress code was designed to make it clear which class a person belonged to.

Upper-class Aztecs wore colorful, decorated clothes that often featured embroidery or feathers. Jewelry made of metal, stone, glass, and other materials was common. Rulers were the only people who dressed more elaborately than people in the upper class. On the lowest end of the class system were slaves. Males wore plain loin cloths, and females wore long skirts with a blouse. Children in all classes dressed similarly to their parents.

A colored woodcut depicts the arrival of Cortés and his men in Tenochtitlán in 1519. The image is based on a nineteenth-century illustration. The splendor and riches of the Aztec Empire are evident from this image.

Montezuma's men offered the rest of the soldiers gifts of food and gold. Then they led the soldiers into the center of the city, where they would camp as guests of the empire. Cortés and his men were amazed by the beauty of Tenochtitlán. The nearly two-hundred-year-old city was often called the City of Dreams. It was filled with towers and temples, clothing and artworks decorated with gold and jewels, statues and weaponry, and pictographs showing Aztec stories, both old and new.

After Montezuma II's death, Cuauhtémoc became the Aztec emperor. This sixteenth-century Spanish painting depicts his capture during the siege against the Aztecs.

Soon Cortés acted to seize control of Tenochtitlán. He stormed the palace and took Montezuma hostage. According to some accounts, Cortés killed Montezuma. Others claim the Aztecs rioted and stoned their ruler to death as punishment for his weak stance against the Spanish invasion. Eventually the unrest among the Aztecs forced Cortés's men to flee. Many were killed or drowned. Cortés returned to Tlaxcala to rebuild his army. Along with his indigenous allies, Cortés built a fleet of small ships. Then the army returned to the weakened Aztec Empire. The siege against the Aztecs lasted from 1519 to 1521. But by August 13, 1521, the once-mighty Aztecs had been defeated. More than two hundred thousand of them died in battle.

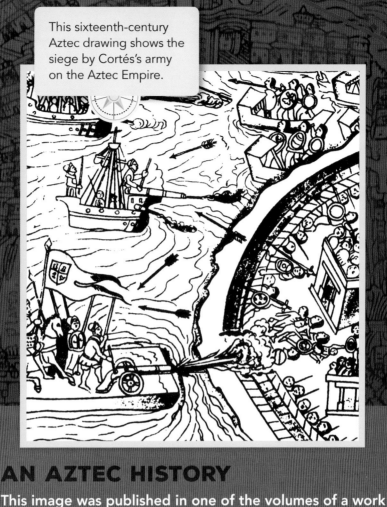

This sixteenth-century Aztec drawing shows the siege by Cortés's army on the Aztec Empire.

AN AZTEC HISTORY

This image was published in one of the volumes of a work known as the *Florentine Codex*. The work, made up of twelve books, tells the history and culture of Mexico. It was put together by Bernardino de Sahagún, a missionary who came to Mexico eight years after the Spanish conquest ended. To gather information, Sahagún asked questions of the indigenous people he met. Some wrote down their answers using pictographs. Sahagún then worked with local indigenous students to interpret and translate the images.

This image shows Spanish conquistadores directing indigenous workers forced to build Mexico City on top of the Aztec ruins.

About his success, Cortés wrote in a letter: "On the day . . . the city was taken, we gathered up all the spoils we could find and returned to our camp, giving thanks to Our Lord for such a favor and the much desired victory which he had granted us."

Cortés ordered his men to erase all traces of the Aztec culture. They toppled buildings, smashed artworks, and burned records. Then when they were finished, they built their new capital on top of the rubble and named it Mexico City.

This Aztec poem, or lament, was written in Nahuatl, an Aztec language, possibly as early as 1528. It brings to life the Aztecs' devastation over the loss of their capital city:

Broken spears lie in the roads;
we have torn our hair in grief.
The houses are roofless now, and their walls
are reddened with blood.

Worms are swarming in the streets and plazas,
and the walls are splattered with gore.
The water has turned red, as if it were dyed,
and when we drink it,
it has the taste of brine.

We have pounded our hands in despair
against the adobe walls,
for our inheritance, our city, is lost and dead.
The shields of our warriors were its defense,
but they could not save it.

We have chewed dry twigs and salt grasses;
we have filled our mouths with dust and bits of adobe;
we have eaten lizards, rats, and worms. . . .

A 1584 portrait of Hernán Cortés, created by André Thevet

CHAPTER 4
CORTÉS'S LATER YEARS

After Cortés's triumph, the Aztec Empire was renamed New Spain. The territory spanned about 80,000 square miles (207,200 square kilometers) from the Caribbean Sea to the Pacific Ocean. It cut through areas of modern central and southern Mexico to Guatemala. Cortés was made governor of New Spain in 1522. But Cortés would never again experience anything close to the kind of success he'd achieved during the Spanish conquest of Mexico. The rest of his career was frustrating for him.

In 1524 he left Mexico City to fight a revolt that had been organized against him in Honduras. Upon his return, he found

This sixteenth-century map shows New Spain. The map was created by Diego Gutiérrez, who was appointed as the official mapmaker for Spanish explorations in 1554.

that the king had removed him as governor. The king refused to change his decision. But Cortés traveled to Spain and spent years trying to regain his authority in Mexico.

Cortés returned to Mexico in 1530 and stayed there for the next ten years. During this time, he led his last major exploration. He and his men established a small Spanish colony in Baja California in northwest Mexico. But indigenous groups there fought hard to drive them away. The founding of the first permanent Spanish settlement there wouldn't happen until 1695, long after Cortés's death.

Hernán Cortés retired to Spain in 1540 and spent much of his time seeking royal recognition for his contributions to his country. His career had made him rich but left him bitter. He died of a lung disease called pleurisy at his estate in Seville on December 2, 1547. He was about sixty-two years old.

Before his death, Cortés asked that his body be buried in a monastery in Mexico. Instead, he was buried in a church in Seville, Spain. Several years later, however, Cortés's remains were dug up and sent to Mexico.

This image depicts Cortés's estate in Seville, Spain.

In the nineteenth century Cortés became a symbol of tragedy for the Native peoples of Mexico. An official at the time, Lucas Alamán, feared that Cortés's remains would be stolen or destroyed, so he said they had been sent to Italy. Instead, he hid Cortés's bones under a beam at the Hospital de Jesus Nazareno in Mexico City.

The Church of the Immaculate Conception and Jesus the Nazarene in the historic center of Mexico City became the final resting place of Hernán Cortés.

This hospital is said to be built at the place where Cortés first met Montezuma II in 1519.

Alamán later moved Cortés's remains behind a wall at the Church of the Immaculate Conception and Jesus the Nazarene. He secretly told the Spanish Embassy so that the remains would not be lost. In 1946 Spanish officials and historians discovered the letter from Alamán to the embassy and confirmed that the bones were real. Cortés's remains are still buried in the church in Mexico City.

WHAT DO YOU THINK?

It's been several centuries since the Spanish conquest of Mexico. In what ways do you think attitudes have changed about conquistadores like Hernán Cortés? Do you think conquistadores are more likely viewed as heroes or villains? Why?

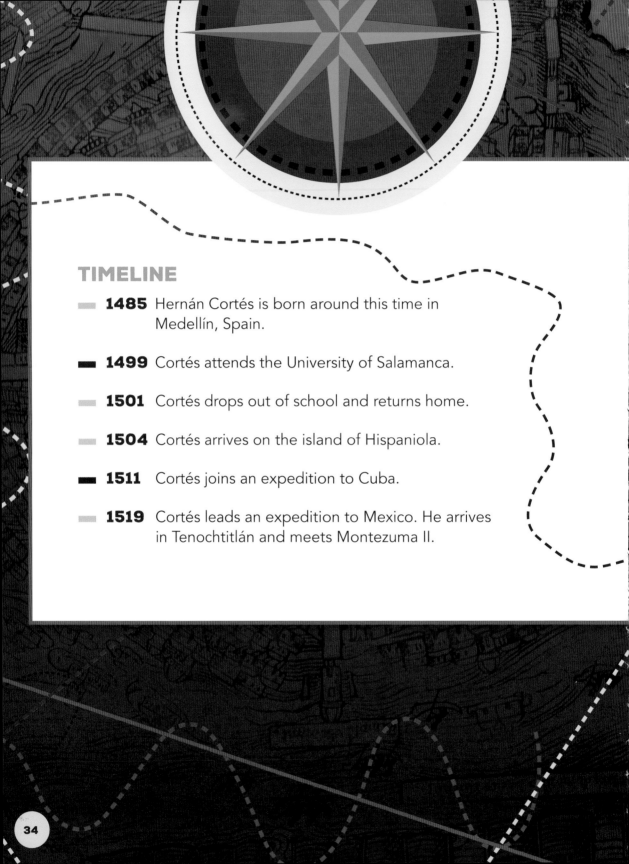

TIMELINE

1485 Hernán Cortés is born around this time in Medellín, Spain.

1499 Cortés attends the University of Salamanca.

1501 Cortés drops out of school and returns home.

1504 Cortés arrives on the island of Hispaniola.

1511 Cortés joins an expedition to Cuba.

1519 Cortés leads an expedition to Mexico. He arrives in Tenochtitlán and meets Montezuma II.

1520 Montezuma II is killed.

1521 Cortés and his men conquer the Aztec Empire.

1528 Cortés returns to Spain.

1530 Cortés returns to Mexico.

1535 On his final expedition, Cortés explores Baja California.

1540 Cortés retires to Spain.

1547 Hernán Cortés dies in Seville.

SOURCE NOTES

4   Hernán Cortés, *Cartas y relaciones de Hernan Cortés al emperador Carlos V.*, ed. Pascual de Gayangos (Paris: A. Chaix, 1866), microfilm, also available at http://bit.ly/29w4YCv.

7   Francisco López de Gómara, *Cortes: The Life of the Conqueror by His Secretary,* trans. and ed. Lesley Byrd Simpson (Berkeley: University of California Press, 1964), 8.

9   Martin W. Sandler, *Atlantic Ocean: The Illustrated History of the Ocean That Changed the World* (New York: Sterling, 2008), 110.

16 Richard Lee Marks, *Cortes: The Great Adventurer and the Fate of Aztec Mexico* (New York: Alfred A. Knopf, 1993), 37.

17 Bernal Díaz del Castillo, *The Discovery and Conquest of Mexico*, trans. A. P. Maudslay (Cambridge, MA: Da Capo, 2003), 2.

28 Buddy Levy, *Conquistador: Hernan Cortez, Montezuma, and the Last Stand of the Aztecs* (New York: Bantam Dell, 2008), Kindle edition, 4681.

29 "The Fall of the Aztecs: Aztec Lament," *PBS*, accessed October 24, 2016, https://www.pbs.org/conquistadors/cortes/cortes_i02.html.

GLOSSARY

ally: a person or group who supports another group of people in a war

causeway: a raised road or path that goes across wet ground or water

expedition: a journey by a group of people who want to explore a distant land

Indies: the islands between North and South America

indigenous: descended from the original occupants of a land before the land was taken over by others

musketeer: a soldier armed with a musket

nobility: members of the upper class in some societies

notary: a public officer who authorizes legal documents

pictograph: an ancient picture or drawing on a rock wall, or a symbol used in writing. Aztecs used a symbolic writing system in their books.

SELECTED BIBLIOGRAPHY

Cortés, Hernán. *Letters from Mexico*. Translated and edited by Anthony Pagden. New Haven, CT: Yale University Press, 1986.

Díaz del Castillo, Bernal. *The Discovery and Conquest of Mexico*. Translated by A. P. Maudslay. Cambridge, MA: Da Capo, 2003.

Levy, Buddy. *Conquistador: Hernan Cortez, King Montezuma, and the Last Stand of the Aztecs*. New York: Bantam Books, 2008.

López de Gómara, Francisco. *Cortes: The Life of the Conqueror by His Secretary*. Translated and edited by Lesley Byrd Simpson. Berkeley: University of California Press, 1964.

Marks, Richard Lee. *Cortes: The Great Adventurer and the Fate of Aztec Mexico*. New York: Alfred A. Knopf, 1993.

Thomas, Hugh. *Conquest: Montezuma, Cortés, and the Fall of Old Mexico*. New York: Simon & Schuster, 1993.

FURTHER INFORMATION

Aztec Empire for Kids
http://aztecs.mrdonn.org/index.html
This site offers a variety of articles about the Aztec Empire.

Bodden, Valerie. *Aztec Warriors*. Mankato, MN: Child's World, 2015. This detail-rich title looks at the history, battles, and training of Aztec warriors.

Doeden, Matt. *The Aztecs: Life in Tenochtitlán*. Minneapolis: Millbrook Press, 2010. This colorfully illustrated book provides a glimpse at ancient Aztecs' everyday lives.

Donaldson, Madeline. *Deadly Bloody Battles*. Minneapolis: Lerner Publications, 2013. This book highlights key moments from several of history's deadliest battles.

Famous Explorers: Hernán Cortés
http://famous-explorers.org/hernan-cortes
This web page presents key biographical information about Hernán Cortés.

Words of Life—Nahuatl, Norte de Puebla
http://globalrecordings.net/en/program/C04461
This collection of MP3 recordings features a form of the Nahuatl language still spoken in the State of Puebla in Mexico.

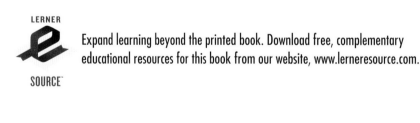

LERNER

Expand learning beyond the printed book. Download free, complementary educational resources for this book from our website, www.lerneresource.com.

SOURCE

INDEX

PHOTO ACKNOWLEDGMENTS

The images in this book are used with the permission of: © Wikimedia Commons (Public Domain) (map background); © Photo Researchers, Inc/Alamy, p. 4; © Lanmas/Alamy, p. 5; © age fotostock/Alamy, p. 6; World Digital Library, p. 7; Library of Congress, p. 7; © Columbus at San Salvador (colour litho), Ferris, Jean Leon Gerome/Bridgeman Images, p. 8; The Granger Collection, New York, pp. 9, 11, 16, 22, 27; © Classic Image/Alamy, p. 10; © Hernando Cortes/Spanish School/Museo de America, Madrid/Spain/Bridgeman Images, p. 12; © Antiqua Print Gallery/Alamy, p. 13; © De Agostini//Getty Images, pp. 14, 15, 24; © Museo de la Ciudad, Mexico/Index/Bridgeman Images, p. 17; © INTERFOTO/Alamy, p. 18; © PRISMA ARCHIVO/ Alamy, p. 20; © Spanish School, (19th century)/Private Collection/ Ken Welsh/Bridgeman Images, p. 21; © Laura Westlund/Independent Picture Service, p. 23; © North Wind Picture Archives/Alamy, pp. 25, 32; © Spanish School, (16th century)/Private Collection/Bridgeman Images, p. 26; © Print Collector/Getty Images, p. 28; © Internet Archive scan of Les vrais pourtraits et vies des hommes illustres grecz, latins et payens/Wikimedia Commons (Public Domain), p. 30; © Photo Researchers, Inc/Alamy, p. 31; © Thelmadatter/ Wikimedia Commons (CC BY-SA 3.0), p. 33.

Front cover: © Cathyrose Melloan/Alamy; © Wikimedia Commons (Public Domain) (map background).